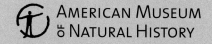

AMERICAN MUSEUM ᵒᶠ NATURAL HISTORY

STERLING CHILDREN'S BOOKS
New York

An Imprint of Sterling Publishing Co., Inc.
1166 Avenue of the Americas
New York, NY 10036

ISBN 978-1-4549-3212-3
Distributed in Canada by Sterling Publishing Co., Inc.
c/o Canadian Manda Group, 664 Annette Street
Toronto, Ontario M6S 2C8, Canada
Distributed in the United Kingdom by GMC Distribution Services
Castle Place, 166 High Street, Lewes, East Sussex BN7 1XU, England
Distributed in Australia by NewSouth Books, 45 Beach Street, Coogee, NSW 2034, Australia

For information about custom editions, special sales, and premium and corporate purchases, please contact Sterling Special Sales at 800-805-5489 or specialsales@sterlingpublishing.com.

Manufactured in China

Lot #:
2 4 6 8 10 9 7 5 3 1
10/18

sterlingpublishing.com

Text written by Ben Richmond

IMAGE CREDITS
Alamy: ©Jurgen Feuerer: 8-9
Getty Images: ©Martin Heigan: 22; ©Chris Johns: 21 (bottom); ©Sergio Pitamitz: 21 (top); ©Diana Robinson: 5, 17 (top); ©Manoj Shah: 23 (top)
iStock: 2630ben: 28-29; Balasclick: 24; Kenneth Canning: 11; Frahaus: 27
Minden Pictures: ©Neil Aldridge/NPL: front endpaper; ©Theo Allofs: 14; ©Karl Ammann/NPL: 7 (top); ©Eric Baccega/NPL: 20; ©Richard Du Toit: back endpaper; ©Gerry Ellis: 10; ©Mitsuaki Iwago: 15, 16-17; ©Gerard Lacz/FLPA: 17 (bottom); ©Alain Mafart-Renodier/Biosphoto: 12-13; ©Hiroya Minakuchi: 26; ©Yva Momatiuk and ©John Eastcott: 19; ©Anup Shah: 25
Nature Picture Library: ©Will Burrard-Lucas: 7 (bottom); ©Klein & Hubert: 18 right (2); ©Andy Rouse: 23 (bottom); ©Anup Shah: 18 (left)

AMERICAN MUSEUM ᵒᶠ NATURAL HISTORY

Baby Elephant Joins the Herd

STERLING CHILDREN'S BOOKS

New York

On a hot day in the African savannah, a baby elephant is born. A baby elephant is called a calf. Newborn African savannah elephants weigh about 200 pounds.

After a couple hours, the calf stands on her feet! The world is a big place—there is much to explore!

The calf joins a group of elephants, called a herd. Members of the herd gather around to meet the newborn. They touch her with their trunks and make trumpet sounds to welcome her into the group. With lions, crocodiles, hyenas, and other predators around, the world can be a dangerous place for a baby elephant. But in the herd, she will be protected.

Herds have anywhere between eight and 30 members.
A herd is made up of several families of elephants and is led by a
matriarch. A matriarch is the largest or oldest female elephant
in the herd. Female elephants are called cows. Most of the adults
in the herd are cows, and they care for the calves together.

Male elephants are called bulls. They live with the herd until they are about ten or twelve. After that, they move away to live with other young bulls. Eventually, they move again to live on their own.

The calf is hungry. She drinks her mother's milk! Calves drink up to three gallons of milk a day for two to ten years. The milk has important nutrients that help calves grow.

The calf's mother is hungry, too! The herd travels single file in search of food. Adult elephants eat up to 300 pounds of food every day. The herd has to keep moving to find enough leaves, roots, grasses, fruits, and bark for all to eat.

At four months old, the calf's trunk is strong enough to pick up small objects. Made of almost 50,000 muscles, including two "fingers" at the end, an elephant's trunk is a very useful tool that helps elephants drink water, pick up food, and dig holes. Adult elephants can lift up to 550 pounds with their trunks!

Elephants also
use their trunks to
greet one another
and to play.

The calf raises her trunk to get the attention of another
young elephant. They touch each other's faces and flap their ears,
a motion that elephants do when they are feeling joyful.

The herd arrives at a lake. Finally, they can drink some water!
African elephants drink up to 40 gallons of water a day and
love to cool down by swimming.

The calf follows her mother into the water.

Splash!

Her mother swims out a little farther, holding her trunk above the water so she can breathe.

Still wet from their swim, members of the herd throw dust all over themselves. The dust acts as sunblock and bug repellent, protecting their skin from burns and bug bites. Elephants also roll around and cover themselves in mud to cool their bodies down from the harsh African heat.

African elephants have amazing hearing and can hear sounds from three miles away. Right now, the herd hears a lion approaching.

The elephants circle up in a tight huddle with the calf in the middle.
They shake their heads, showing off their tusks and making
their ears and trunks flap. They also make loud sounds.
The lion leaves—the calf is safe!

At one year old, the baby teeth that the calf was born with fall out. They are replaced with permanent tusks that will grow about seven inches per year throughout her entire life. She uses these tusks to dig up food and water. Tusks also help to scare away predators.

At 15 years old, the calf has become a full-grown adult. She now weighs about three tons, or about 6,000 pounds.

When a new calf is born, the adult elephant gathers with her herd. Together, with flapping ears and loud trumpet sounds, they welcome their newest member.

My name is **Eleanor Hoeger**, and I am a Senior Museum Specialist in the Mammalogy Department at the American Museum of Natural History. I work behind the scenes caring for all the mammal specimens you don't see in the exhibits, including elephants. These specimens help researchers from all over the world learn more about the lives of elephants. For example, did you know that elephants are so heavy they can't jump?